Cartridge Carbines of the British Army

Alan M. Petrillo

Dedication

For my daughter, Lisa, whose smiling outlook on life continually makes me proud.

Other books by Alan M. Petrillo from Excalibur Publications:
British Service Rifles and Carbines 1888-1900
The Lee Enfield Number 1 Rifles
The Lee Enfield Number 4 Rifles
The Number 5 Jungle Carbine

Published by Excalibur Publications
PO Box 36, Latham, NY 12110-0036

ISBN # 1-880677-13-X

First printing — March, 1998

Contents

Snider Carbines

Like most other countries in the mid-19th century, Great Britain entered into a search for a breechloading system with which to arm its military forces. After trying many different systems, the government decided to convert large quantities of the Pattern 1853 family of arms to breechloaders and to continue the search for a more suitable breechloading arm. The conversion system used was developed by Jacob Snider, an American. Both cavalry and artillery models were produced.

The Snider system, adopted in 1867, was a simple modification of the original breechloading arm. It consisted of cutting off the rear portion of the barrel that had included the percussion bolster and breech plug. The rear of the barrel was then threaded on the exterior and screwed into a cylinder-shaped piece of iron that had the top milled out to accept the breech block.

This breech block was hinged on the right side of the action by a rod that passed through an enlargement of the receiver at the front and at the rear. It was held in place by a screw, on the front receiver enlargement, that entered from the top and passed through the rod. Surrounding the rod was a coil spring covered by a two-piece sleeve. The breech block hinge lug had the extractor assembly inserted into it and was operated by pulling the breech block sharply to the rear after opening. The breech block was swung up to the right to open the action by a protrusion on the left side of the block.

A passage for a firing pin was bored through the breech block from a raised bolster on the upper right rear of the block and came out at the front center of the block. The firing pin was held into this block by what looked like a percussion nipple. This screwed into the raised bolster and retained the firing pin and its spring.

The rear of the receiver was closed off by a modified

breech plug. This plug had a hole bored from the rear that came out in the center of its front face. A spring loaded plunger in the hole kept the breech block closed by engaging an indentation in the rear. Arms with this system of breech assembly were designated Mark I, I*, II*, and II**. Each different Mark had minor improvements made to make the action more usable. All of these arms were conversions of percussion arms.

After a series of accidents where the breechblock was blown open by a ruptured cartridge case, a locking device activated by a thumb-operated catch on the left side of the breech block was fitted. This improvement was carried out in 1869. This cammed a locking bolt in the breech block out of a hole bored in the face of the breech plug. Arms fitted with this device were designated Mark III. All Mark III arms were manufactured as new arms rather then as conversions from muzzleloaders.

Changes also were required to the percussion lock. The hammer face was twisted to the left and shortened. On Mark II pattern arms the face of the hammer was cupped out, similar to its original percussion form. On the others it was left flat.

Production of these carbines was carried out at Enfield and also by the Birmingham and London gunmakers. Birmingham Small Arms, London Small Arms, and C.G. Bonehill were the major non-government producers.

Snider Artillery Carbines

With the adoption of the Snider system to convert the obsolete Pattern 1853 family of arms to breechloaders, the British military took a step towards modernizing its forces. For the Royal Artillery this would lead to the production of three different Artillery Carbines. One of these was a straight conversion of the existing Pattern 1861 Artillery Carbine, the other a newly produced arm, and the third a conversion of the Snider Mark III Long Rifle.

The Pattern 1861 Artillery Carbine that formed the basis for the conversion and served as a pattern for the newly-produced carbines shared many features with the other members of the Pattern 1853 family. It was an updated version of the Pattern 1853, and Pattern 1858 Muzzleloading Artillery Carbines.

This carbine had a 24-inch .577 caliber barrel of a five groove pattern with a twist of 1 turn in 48 inches. The barrel was held to the stock by two screw-clamping bands.

The Snider Artillery Carbine Mark II* was approved on May 2, 1867.

The rear band was an improved design of the Baddeley Patent style that completely enclosed the clamping screw and prevented it from catching on clothing or injuring the user's hand. The front band also mounted the sling swivel.

A rearsight graduated to 600 yards, consisting of a base and ladder with a slide for adjusting the range, was fitted near the breech end of the barrel. The front sight, lo cated near the muzzle, consisted of a barleycorn on a block.

The forestock housed the rammer, a rod with an enlarged head that was conically recessed at the front, as well as grooved and slotted to form a cleaning jag to push the Minie projectile down the bore.

A percussion lock was fitted on the right side of the stock, held in place by two bolts. The heads of these bolts rested in brass cup-shaped receptacles. A protrusion on each side of these cups kept them from turning in the stock.

A brass buttplate was mounted at the rear of the stock by three screws. The trigger guard, also of brass, had a small steel screw eye fitted in front of the bow that served to mount the chain to hold the snap cap to the arm. A rear sling swivel mounted on a wood screw was affixed to the lower rear of the buttstock.

Most of the Pattern 1861 Artillery Carbines were put into store for conversion to breechloaders when a suitable system was adopted.

Production of the Mark II** Snider Artillery Carbine was approved on May 2, 1867. Most conversions were made from the Pattern 1861 Artillery Carbine, but a few Pattern 1853s also were used in the conversion program.

The conversion process was rather straightforward, consisting of cutting off a section of the rear of the barrel, threading the end and screwing it into the new breech action. This action was marked with the Roman numerals II** on the front ring.

Slight inletting changes were required at the breech end of the stock to accommodate the larger diameter of the

Most Snider Artillery Carbine Mark II* conversions were from the Pattern 1861 Artillery Carbine.

new action. With the hammer modified to hit the firing pin and the springs suitably adjusted, the lock was reinstalled and the conversion was complete.

The same sword bayonet was used with the new Snider carbine as had been issued with its muzzleloading predecessors. Everything else, such as sights, swivels, and stock furniture, remained unchanged.

By 1869, with the supply of Pattern 1861 Artillery Carbines running low, the government decided to produce a new artillery carbine using the improved Mark III action and all new parts. With the exception of the Mark III action, this new carbine looked the same as the Mark II**. It can be quickly distinguished by the locking bolt latch on the breech block and the Roman numeral III stamped into the front ring of the action.

Production of the Mark III Artillery Carbine continued into the 1880s to meet colonial government orders. The carbines proved to be very popular with the many volunteer artillery companies formed in Great Britain and the colonies, and this served to keep them in production well after the introduction of the Martini-Henry .450 Artillery Carbines.

Even after production of the Mark III Artillery Carbine

ended, there was a strong demand for this type of arm from Cadet Corps and colonial governments. To satisfy this demand the Snider Artillery Carbine Mark IV was developed. First put into production in 1885 for issue to Cadet Corps, it was officially designated the Snider Artillery Carbine Mark IV in 1891. This carbine saw service with many colonial volunteer units, as well as issue in Great Britain. This was three years after the new Lee-Metford magazine system was adopted and 14 years after the Martini-Henry Artillery Carbines were put into production to supplant the Snider arms.

This carbine differed from the other Artillery Carbines in that it was a conversion from either Pattern 1853 Long Rifle or Snider Long Rifle. While this design used the Mark III action, a Mark III Snider Artillery Carbine already existed so the Mark was advanced to IV. The conversion process was a little more complex than the previous models since it required shortening the original three-

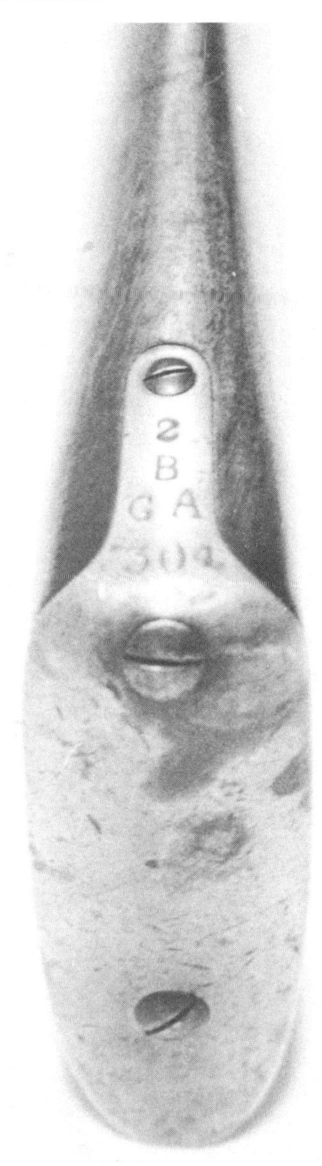

The brass buttplate tang on this Artillery Carbine bears the British Army stampings that designate the weapon's assigned regiment and other details, such as the rack number.

This Mark II** Snider Artillery Carbine shows the Snider patent marking, as well as the British broad arrow on the breech block.

groove barrel from 36.5 inches to 22.55 inches, and in the case of a muzzleloading Pattern 1853, fitting of a Snider action.

The stock was then cut to leave the barrel protruding 1-1/8 inches and the nosecap was refitted. A new upper band with a bayonet lug on its right side was then fitted. The band also carried the front sling swivel. The rear swivel was removed from the trigger guard, the hole filled and a new swivel on a screw stud positioned to the rear of the trigger guard. A small steel screw stud was installed in front of the trigger guard and used to attach the chain that held the snapcap.

The rearsight was a modified Long Rifle sight, graduated to 900 yards. But the original markings were removed and the new 900 yard marking was considerably lower on the leaf than on the Long Rifle sight.

The normal Artillery Carbine bayonet would not fit these carbines and a slightly modified Pattern 1858 Sword Bayonet was used, housed in a steel Artillery pattern scabbard.

Snider Cavalry Carbines

The Mark III Snider Cavalry Carbine went into production in 1869.

The British Army had long sought a breechloading carbine for its mounted units, which had led them through a bewildering search for the perfect system. Three types of breechloaders received widespread use in British service — the Sharps, the Calisher and Terry, and the Westley Richards "Monkeytail." But only the Westley Richards carbine was produced in any quantity and it was quickly superseded by more modern breechloading cartridge arms.

To supplement these breechloading carbines a muzzleloading carbine designed as part of the Pattern 1853 family of arms was produced. Originally made for issue in India, its use was later expanded to other British units. Produced in two types — designated Pattern 1856 and Pattern 1861 — it would, like the other Pattern 1853 family of arms, form the basis for the first breechloading cartridge arms used in large numbers by the British.

As first introduced, the Pattern 1856 Cavalry Carbine

was a .577 caliber, percussion muzzleloading arm. It was stocked nearly to the muzzle and carried a rammer in the forestock that was attached to the barrel by a swivel arrangement to keep it from being lost when loading on horseback. The 21-inch barrel was held to the stock by two bands.

A two-leaf rearsight was fitted near the breech, while a barleycorn frontsight on a block was mounted near the muzzle. Rifling was three grooves with a 1 in 78 inch twist.

The percussion lock was held to the stock by two bolts passing through the stock from the left side. The bolts also secured the sling bar and ring to the stock. The buttplate, trigger guard and muzzle cap were brass, while the barrel bands and sling bar and ring were iron. A small iron screw eye, on the trigger guard in front of the bow, was used to affix the chain that held the snap cap to the carbine.

In 1861 the carbine pattern was modified. A new rearsight, consisting of a base and a ladder with a slide and adjustable to 600 yards, was fitted. The barrel bands were changed to the new Baddeley Patent style, designed to enclose the clamping screw and prevent it from catching on clothing or injuring the user's hand. In addition, the rifling was changed to a five groove 1 in 48 inch twist bore. A few Pattern 1861 Carbines were produced without the sling bar and ring.

By the time that the Pattern 1861 Carbine was put into production the government had decided to move towards a new family of breechloading cartridge arms. Most of the newly-completed arms were put into store to await conversion. In 1866 the British Army adopted a design based on the Jacob Snider's system.

Snider Cavalry Carbines were produced in three versions — Mark II**, Mark III, and the Snider Yeomanry Carbine Mark I. The conversion of Pattern 1861 Cavalry Carbines to Snider Cavalry Carbines was started in 1867, using the Mark II** action.

Conversion resulted in an arm that did not look like the

original Pattern 1861 Carbine and was quite different from other Snider arms. The stock was shortened to a half stock configuration and the ramrod hole was filled. Only the lower band was retained to hold the barrel in the stock. To keep the band from sliding forward under recoil, a pin was installed through the stock in front of the band.

Provision for a cleaning rod was made in the rear of the buttstock by boring a recess to house a two-piece rod with a cleaning jag at one end and a ball to serve as a handle at the other. These two pieces screwed together to make a rod of suitable length to clean the barrel. It was retained in the stock by a hinged trap in the brass buttplate.

The rearsight was graduated to 600 yards and protected by a leather cover held on the stock by two wood screws. The screws were located on each side of the stock and one served as a button over which a slot in the leather cover fastened. The other screw attached the cover firmly to the stock, but allowed it to swivel and un-

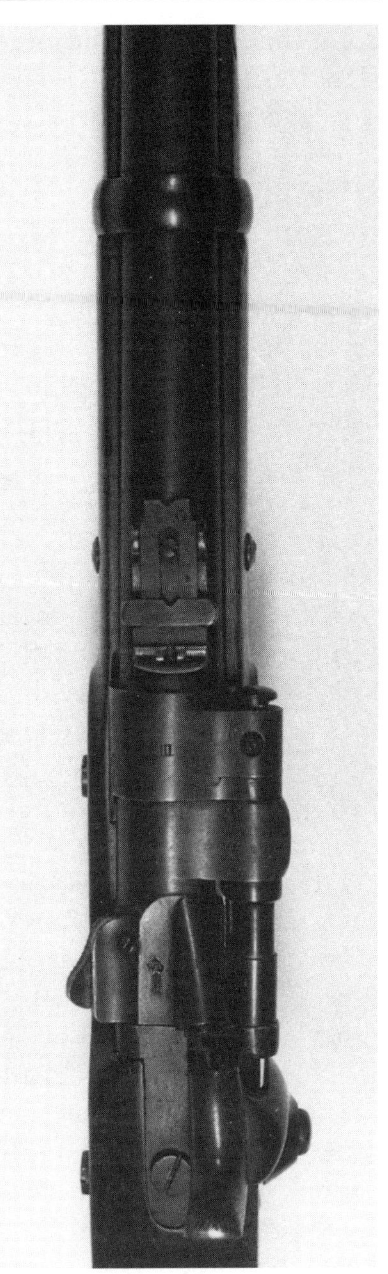

The distinctive carbine rearsight, graduated to 600 yards, is apparent on this Mark III Snider Cavalry Carbine.

cover the rearsight. The foresight was the same as used on the Pattern 1861 Cavalry Carbine.

The original sling bar and ring were retained on most of the carbines of the Mark II** pattern. Some Pattern 1861 Cavalry Carbines and Snider Mark II** Cavalry Carbines were built without sling bars and rings.

By 1869 all suitable Pattern 1861 Cavalry Carbines had been converted and production was continued using new components. By this time the improved Mark III locking action had been adopted and was employed in building the new arm, which was put into production in 1869.

The new stock did not have the wood filler in the ramrod groove at the forend, as it too was of new construction. Another change occurred when the decision to use steel barrels was made at about the same time as the new Mark III action was put into production. Very few Mark III Carbines were produced with the original iron barrels.

Some Mark III Carbines will be found fitted with the sling bar and ring on the side of the stock, while others have a sling ring and stud fitted to the rear of the trigger guard. Large numbers of Mark III Carbines were built without sling attachments of any form, and these generally have brass, side bolt cups. These carbines were designed to be carried in saddle scabbards.

One other form of carbine was built on the Snider Cavalry Carbine pattern. Originally a Snider Long Rifle, it became the Snider Yeomanry Carbine Mark I.

This arm was fabricated to meet the demands of the volunteer cavalry units at a time when the major arms producers were busy producing Martini-Henry arms. Approved on July 19, 1880, this carbine was a conversion of Mark II** and Mark III Snider Long Rifles. The conversion consisted of cutting back the barrel to 19.25 inches, shortening the stock, plugging the ramrod hole, fitting a new carbine rearsight and foresight, installing a leather sight cover, modifying the buttstock to take the two-piece cleaning rod, and fitting a steel screw

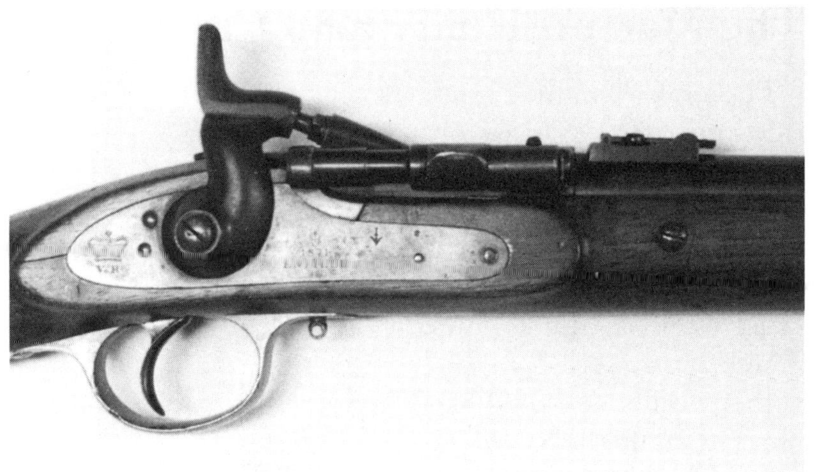

Three versions of the Snider Artillery Carbine were produced — the Mark II**, the Mark III and the Yeomanry Carbine Mark I. This Mark III used the improved locking system.

eye to affix the snapcap chain.

Two differences from the standard pattern cavalry carbines were apparent in these conversions. Since the forend of the original Long Rifle was one inch longer from breech to lower band, the Snider Yeomanry Carbine Mark I is one inch longer. In addition, the bore retains the three groove, 1 turn in 78 inches of the original pattern.

Production of Snider Cavalry Carbines continued into the 1880s to meet demand from colonial forces and police. They remained in use in various areas of the Empire into the early years of the 20th century.

The Martini-Henry .450 Carbines

The .450 Martini-Henry rifles proved to be satisfactory arms for the infantry and rifle units of the British and colonial forces, but were not considered suitable for issue to cavalry and artillery units. These units were equipped with specially designed carbines based on the Snider action, and new patterns based on the Martini-Henry action were considered desirable.

Development of the carbine versions of the Martini-Henry series occurred at the same time as that of the rifles. As an improvement was made in either the rifle or carbine, that improvement was normally applied to the other version. No carbine versions of the Martini-Henry Mark IV were introduced.

Versions of the carbine were produced for issue to cavalry, garrison artillery, field artillery, and horse artillery. These carbines were also issued to colonial, militia, volunteer units, police, and later used widely as drill purpose arms like the various patterns of rifles.

The Martini-Henry Carbine Mark I was approved on December 1, 1877.

The Martini-Henry Carbine Mark I

A carbine version of the Martini-Henry was approved for service on December 1, 1877. This carbine was intended to be suitable for use by the cavalry, garrison artillery, horse artillery, and field artillery. It would, in fact, replace the cavalry and artillery carbine patterns of the Snider system with one arm. Soon after the introduction of the Mark I carbine, it was realized that one pattern would not serve to meet the needs of both the cavalry and artillery.

After prolonged development problems, primarily relating to excessive recoil of the rifle cartridge in the much lighter carbine, a new reduced load cartridge was introduced. This cartridge used a 410-grain bullet with 70 grains of black powder, instead of the more potent rifle loading of a 480-grain bullet with 85 grains of powder. Trials showed this cartridge to be pleasant to shoot, and in an emergency either the carbine or rifle cartridge could be used in either arm.

This new carbine resembled the rifle in many ways. The buttstock was almost identical to the rifle. the only difference being the deletion of the lower sling swivel.

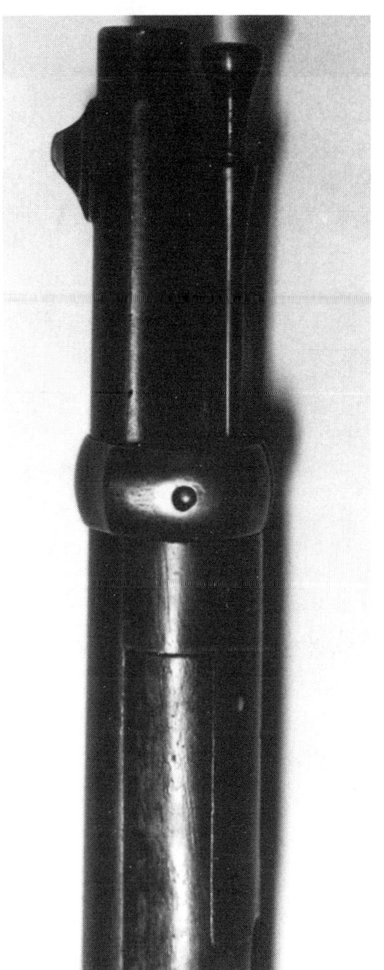

The muzzle of the Mark I shows its design for cavalry use.

The carbine action differed from the Martini-Henry Mark II rifle action only in minor ways. The receiver body was

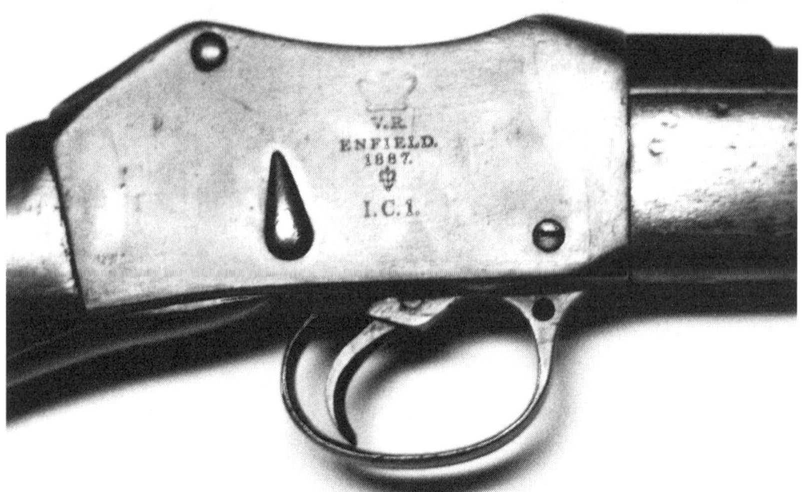

The markings on the right side of the receiver identify this Martini-Henry Mark I Carbine as being made at Enfield in 1887.

rounded off at the lower forward corners to improve entry into the saddle buckets used by the cavalry. The head of the cocking indicator was also reduced in size, and this is quite noticeable when compared with that on the rifle.

Internally the breech block differed from that of the Mark II rifle. It was made wider at the front to steady its movement in the receiver and was fitted with a new striker assembly. The extractor also differs from the Mark II. The cutouts needed to clear the safety that had been fitted to the earliest Martini-Henry Mark I rifles were dispensed with and the lower arm was now solid. In 1885 a new stronger extractor was developed and may be found fitted to earlier carbines and rifles. Such arms are marked "S X" on the receiver ring.

The carbine forend was attached to the receiver by a hook arrangement that engaged a recess in the lower front of the receiver, rather then the stud and pin arrangement of the rifle. This hook was a flat steel strap inlet into the bottom rear of the forend and held there by two wood screws. At its rear was a raised lip that hooked into the receiver's recess.

Barrels of the carbine were 21.375 inches long, and the breech form was changed. The knoxform had a matching projection on the bottom of the barrel, which made a stronger breech assembly.

The foresight was a fine barleycorn, and had wings added on both sides to protect it from wear when being put in the saddle bucket.

The rear sight was sighted to 1,180 yards over the top of the leaf cap, and up to 1,000 yards on the leaf itself. The sight bed, marked from 100 to 400 yards, was attached to the barrel by a dovetail at the front and a screw at the rear, instead of being soldered to the barrel as was done on the rifle.

Two bands secured the forend to the barrel. The rear one was located about halfway back from the muzzle. It was split at the bottom and secured with a screw that applied a clamping action to it. The upper band was wider and solid, secured by a pin that passed through it and the nosecap.

At the front of the forend was a nosecap, held by two

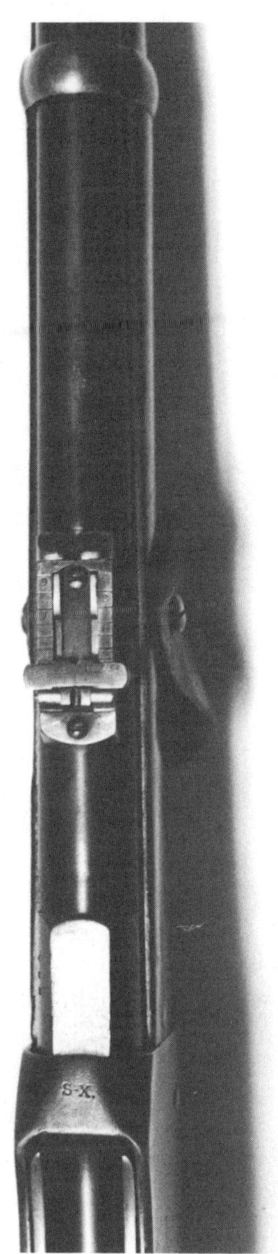

The S X on the receiver ring of this Martini-Henry Mark I Carbine designates a stronger extractor developed in 1885.

screws that passed through the forend from the inside of the barrel channel on each side of the cleaning rod channel. The nosecap extended forward on the barrel to a point just below the front sight. It was scalloped in front of the band and served to support the front of the cleaning rod. The nosecap also contained a raised lip that retained the cleaning rod.

A channel was cut into the stock, running back from the nosecap to the rear band. Then a hole was bored through the rest of the forend to contain the cleaning rod.

In 1879, a leather rear sight cover was approved for issue. This required a wood screw to be installed on each side of the forend below the rear sight to attach the cover to the forend. After the initial introduction, the heads of the screws were rounded off to reduce the chance of snagging or cutting the uniforms of the users.

The cleaning rod for the carbine was 21 inches long and swelled out at the front with a sharp shoulder formed near the front to engage the rod catch on the nosecap. It then extended forward a short distance before ending in a bulbous tip. The lower end was threaded to fit a cleaning jag.

This then was the Carbine, Martini-Henry, Mark I as originally produced for use by cavalry and artillery units. Changes to this carbine were made from time to time as improvements were developed or needs changed. These included the fixing of a leather cover for the rear sight, as previously noted, the modification of the forend hook, and the addition of a sling swivel to the heel of the buttstock. This was to allow the use of a sling with the carbine. The sling attached to the upper end of the carbine with a leather loop.

Mark I carbines may be found with other modifications, such as the addition of a sling swivel to the upper band, allowing the use of a normal style sling.

Martini-Henry Garrison Artillery Carbine

Shortly after the introduction of the Mark I carbine it was decided that it would not serve the needs of the garrison artillery and modifications to the existing carbine were proposed. It was felt that the garrison artillery required a carbine that would fix a bayonet. As produced, the Mark I Carbine could not fix a bayonet.

Ultimately, the decision was taken to modify the Mark I carbine to fix a sword bayonet. The bayonet itself was to be modified from the Yataghan bayonet used on the Snider artillery carbines. The only change needed was to the bushing of the muzzle ring of the bayonet to accommodate the smaller diameter Martini-Henry barrel.

This bayonet was to be fixed only in emergencies, since it was felt that the combination was too short to be of much real use. When the Garrison Artillery Carbine was issued in 1878, it was done with out the bayonets since a new bayonet was under development for use on the Martini-Henry artillery carbines.

To fit the bayonet, the following modifications were required. A new nose band with a bayonet lug on its right side was fitted, similar to the one found on the Martini-Henry rifles. The length of the bayonet's hilt required that this band also be moved fur-

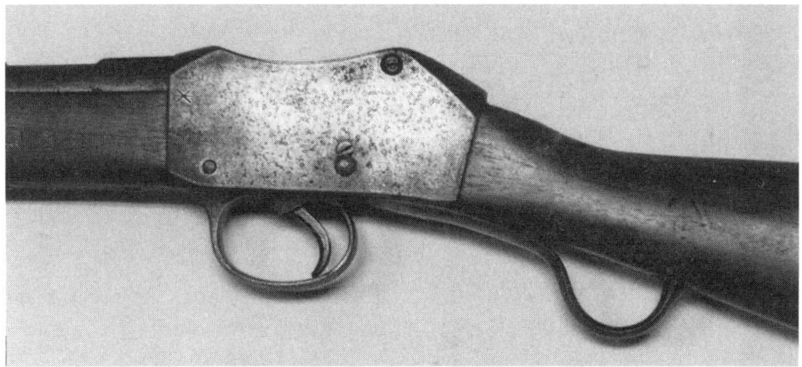

The Garrison Artillery Carbine was first issued in 1878.

ther from the muzzle so that the bayonet's muzzle ring could fit over the carbine's muzzle. Modifications to the cleaning rod also were required.

The rod on the original Mark I carbine extended to a point even with the muzzle of the gun. In order for the bayonet to be fitted, the rod had to be shortened to provide the required clearance for the bayonet cross guard. The shape of the end of the cleaning rod was changed at the same time, and took the form of a sphere rather then the tulip shaped tip used on the Mark I Carbine.

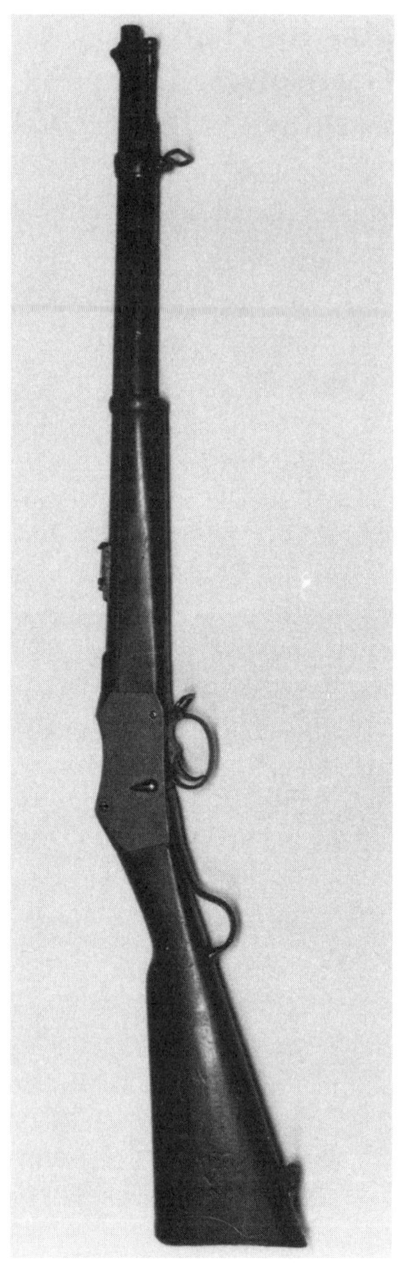

The Martini-Henry Artillery Carbine Mark I was desiged as an arm that could fix a bayonet.

The Martini-Henry Artillery Carbine Mark I

While the Garrison Artillery Carbine was being developed it was decided that all of the artillery units — garrison, field, and horse, should have a carbine that fixed a bayonet. While the garrison artillery did not require a sling, it was decided that the field and horse artillery did require one. This new pattern of carbine was approved for production

The Mark I Artillery Carbine's development changed the nomenclature of all British carbines.

in April of 1878.

The new carbine was fitted with sling swivels. One was located on the heel of the buttstock, 2-1/4 inches from the toe, while the other was located on the bottom of the upper band.

The upper band also carried the bayonet lug on its right side like the Garrison Artillery Carbine. But the lug had its front edge rounded off, to prevent injury to the user's hand.

Cleaning rods for the new Artillery Carbine were similar in length to the Garrison Artillery Carbine rod, but had a tulip-shaped head with a recess in its front surface. This recess was designed to clear the firing pin tip if the rod was dropped down the bore with the gun in an uncocked state.

The nomenclature of all carbines was changed as a result of the development of the Mark I Artillery Carbine. It was decided that the word "Garrison" would be discontinued, since all artillery units were to be equipped with the new carbine. In addition, the original Mark I Carbine for all services was to be known as the Martini-Henry Carbine Cavalry Mark I. These changes took place in 1879.

Bayonets for the new carbine were the subject of much debate. Eventually two patterns were accepted into service. These were the modified Pattern 1860 sword bayonet with bushed muzzle ring (similar to the pattern originally adopted for the Garrison Artillery Carbine), and the Artillery Carbine Bayonet Mark I or Pattern 1879 sword bayonet.

Martini-Henry Artillery Carbine Mark II

With the adoption of the .303 Cartridge and the Lee-Metford series of arms in 1888, the days of the .450 Martini-Henry should have been numbered. In an effort to save money and equip as many of the British forces with the new .303 arms the decision was made to convert .450 Martini arms into .303 rifles and carbines suitable for issue to units not requiring the new magazine arms.

Large quantities of .450 arms and ammunition still remained in British stores. By the 1890s, the newer models of Martini-Henry arms were being converted to .303. This left a need for arms to fill the gap left by their withdrawal from service.

To fill this need, it was decided to take Martini-Henry

The Martini-Henry Artillery Carbine Mark II was approved on August 18, 1891.

Mark II rifles and convert them to a new pattern of artillery carbine. This arm was known as the Martini-Henry Artillery Carbine Mark II. It was approved on August 18, 1891 for use by Volunteer Artillery units and Colonial forces. The use of the Mark II rifle to produce this carbine resulted in their classification as second class arms, since the Mark IIs had been downgraded with the adoption of the Mark III arms.

The conversion was straightforward, but at the same time provided a serviceable arm at minimum cost. The rifle barrel was shortened to 21.35 inches, and the muzzle diameter reduced to allow the fixing of a bayonet.

The foresight was attached to the muzzle and was of a standard rifle pattern rather than the carbine version with side wings. To protect the foresight, a special brass fore sight protector was designed and issued. A carbine pattern rear sight was soldered to the barrel, and the original rifle sight mounting holes were filled.

The rifle forend was shortened and the retaining shoulders for the bands moved to the rear. The hole for the rear band retaining pin was filled and new holes drilled for retaining pins for both bands. The nosecap was also refitted. The new forend was designed to come within 1 inch of the muzzle.

Modifications to the bands also were required. Both had the inside diameter expanded to accept the larger diameter of the barrel at their new locations. The upper band retained the sling swivel originally fitted when the arm was a rifle.

A marking disk was fitted to the buttstock to allow unit identifications to be placed on the carbine. A lower sling swivel was fitted to the lower rear of the buttstock to allow the fitting of a sling. All markings pertaining to the original Mark II rifle configuration were removed from the right side of the butt stock, and new markings were stamped in their place.

The receiver also was modified by fitting the Mark III extractor. This can be identified by the "S-X" stamped into the top of the receiver ring or by disassembling the action. The right side of the receiver retained the original rifle markings, while the new designation "MH .45" over "AC II" was stamped on the left side of the receiver. Not all Mark II Artillery Carbines seem to have been marked, and specimens may be found without these markings.

A new cleaning rod was designed for the Mark II Artillery Carbine. It is similar to the Mark II rifle rod, but shorter. No slot is cut in its head and the retaining groove is part of the swelled head rather then being located on a swell to the rear of the head. The lower end of the rod is threaded to accept a jag.

Production of these arms continued into the late 1890s. After their service with the Volunteer Artillery and other units many of the Mark II carbines were passed on to cadet corps along with other obsolete arms. At this time they were frequently marked with a "DP" on the butt stock and on the knoxform of the barrel. In addition a steel marking disk is usually fitted in place of the brass marking disk.

The bayonet used on the Mark II Artillery Carbine was the Pattern 1860 Sword Bayonet that had been used on Enfield muzzleloading short rifles and the later

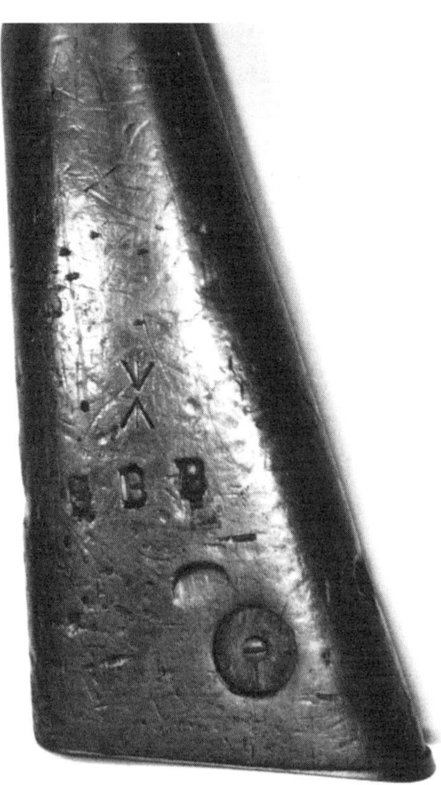

The buttstock on this Martini-Henry Artillery Carbine Mark II carries several markings, including the double broad arrow sale stamp.

Snider conversion short rifles, and later modified for the Mark I and other Martini-Henry rifles. This modification consisted of bushing the muzzle ring for the smaller diameter barrel of the .450 rifles.

Martini-Henry Artillery Carbine Mark III

A second artillery carbine conversion was adopted on September 2, 1891. This carbine differed from the Mark II Artillery Carbine in several features, although externally both carbines look quite similar.

This carbine used the action of the Martini-Henry Carbine Mark I with its rounded off lower front corners. It also employed the lighter carbine barrel with the built in front sight protectors, but with the same rear sight as fitted to the Mark II Artillery Carbine.

Unlike the Mark I pattern carbines, the Mark III used a modified Mark III rifle forend. This was necessary because of the use of the later carbine or Mark III rifle style

The Mark III version of the Martini-Henry Artillery Carbine was the last in the series.

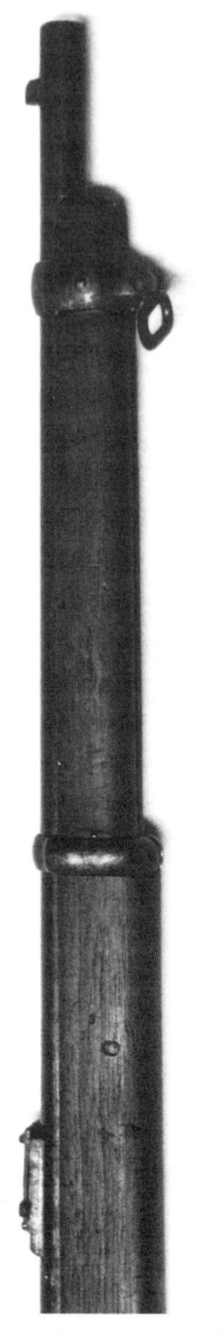

The distance from the muzzle to the forend nosecap wss increased by an inch on the Martini-Henry Mark III Artillery Carbine.

of receiver that featured a hook retained forend. Modifications were similar to those used on the Mark II rifle forend for the Mark II Artillery Carbine. These included repositioning the bands and refitting the nosecap. The distance from the muzzle to the forend nosecap was two inches instead of one inch as on the Mark II Artillery Carbine.

This difference in forends resulted in the need for a different cleaning rod. While both rods were 21 inches in length, the shorter forend of the Mark III Artillery Carbine resulted in the locking groove for the cleaning rod being placed one inch further to the rear.

Production of the Mark III Artillery Carbine appears to have been very limited. Possibly only prototypes were assembled to guide conversion of Mark III rifle type actions into artillery carbines if needed.

Bayonets for the Mark III Artillery Carbine would have been similar to those produced for the Mark I Artillery Carbine.

Martini-Metford Carbines

The British Army has never been known to be wasteful with its arms, and nowhere can it be better illustrated than the vast numbers of Martini-Henry .577/.450 rifles and carbines that were converted to .303 Martini-Metford carbines. These conversions were necessitated by the introduction of the .303 Lee-Metford Magazine Rifle Mark I.

While several rifle and carbine variations were altered in the conversion program to correspond with the new designations, the sighting on the converted arms reflected the chief difference from their predecessors. Those arms converted from the later-produced .303 Martini-Henry Mark V and Mark VI rifles showed a major change back to the barleycorn foresight and V-notch rearsight used in years past, discarding the Lewes sights found on the Mark V and VI.

In 1891, after the cordite .303 round was approved for use, sights on Martini-Metford arms that were designed for the service black powder cartridge again had to be altered.

Seemingly minor adjustment, such as the addition of foresight wings, were debated, tested, debated again, and eventually discontinued.

But while changes and modifications were the order of the day, thousands of rifles and carbines were converted to the new marks, and they went on to provide yeoman's service to the British and colonial soldiers who used them in the service of Queen and country.

Martini-Metford Cavalry Carbines

Five versions of the Martini-Metford Cavalry Carbine were produced, all converted from Martini-Henry arms — four from carbines and one from a rifle. The Henry Rifle Barrel Company, London, (its marking was HRB), in 1891 was awarded the contract for the conversion of 12,000 Martini-Henry Mark I Cavalry Carbines to the Martini-Metford Cavalry Carbine Mark I.

Subsequently, due to a shortage of Martini-Henry Mark I Cavalry Carbines, it was decided to convert 600 carbines from the Martini-Henry Artillery Carbine Mark I. These arms were to be designated the Martini-Metford Cavalry Carbine Mark II, which was issued to horse and field artillery, while the Martini-Metford Cavalry Carbine Mark I was issued to cavalry.

Martini-Metford Cavalry Carbine Mark I

Approved on May 2, 1892, this carbine was converted from the Martini-Henry Mark I Cavalry Carbine. Many of the Martini-Henry cavalry carbine parts were used in the conversion without alteration; however, the upper band, forend hook, nosecap, and forend required some alteration to suit the converted pattern.

In the converted carbine, the Martini-Henry upper band was cut, the forend hook had the rod nut brazed on, the nosecap was shortened, and the forend was cut to accommodate the rod nut.

New components for the Martini-Metford Cavalry Carbine Mark I, supplied by Henry Rifle Barrel Co., were:

- barrel
- block
- foresight and rearsight components
- mainspring
- rod nut
- extractor
- cleaning rod
- various screws.

Length of the carbine was 3 feet one inch, weight was 8 pounds one ounce, and barrel length 21 inches.

Martini-Metford Cavalry Carbine Mark II

The Martini-Metford Cavalry Carbine Mark II was approved on the same date as the Martini-Metford Cavalry Carbine Mark I, and differed very little from that carbine. However, it was converted from a Martini-Henry Artillery Carbine Mark I.

The Mark II differed from the first carbine mark in that the butt swivel hole was plugged, the upper band was cut and drilled to receive the upper band screw and also had the lugs and sword bar removed, and the nosecap was shortened and drilled to receive the upper band screw.

Further, a number of additions were made to the Mark II — a rearsight cover and cover screws were installed, and a screw was added to the upper band.

Length of the carbine was 3 feet one inch, weight was 8 pounds four ounces, and barrel length was 21 inches.

Martini-Metford Cavalry Carbine Mark I* and II*

Complaints from the troops that the about the lack of foresight protecting wings caused a decision to be approved on December 5, 1892 to fit such wings to any carbines manufactured in the future. As such, the Mark I and Mark II Martini-Metford Cavalry Carbines then were manufactured as the Mark I* and Mark II* models.

Length of the carbine was 3 feet one inch, weight was 8 pounds four ounces, and barrel length was 21 inches.

Martini-Metford Cavalry Carbine Mark III

The Martini-Metford Cavalry Carbine Mark III, approved on July 29, 1892, was converted from the Martini-Henry Rifle Mark II. As such, the barrel and forend had to be shortened to the carbine pattern, the sighting had to be altered, the bands changed, and modifications made to the action body.

Many of the rifle's parts were able to be used in the conversion, notably the body, butt and butt plate, cocking indicator, lever and associated parts, trigger and its parts, tumbler, and various screws.

New components included the barrel, foresight, rearsight, cleaning rod, extractor, block, forend, nosecap, marking disc, striker, mainspring, and various screws and pins.

Length of the carbine was 3 feet one inch, weight was 6 pounds 12 ounces, and barrel length was 21 inches.

Martini-Metford Artillery Carbines

Four versions of the Martini-Metford Artillery Carbine were produced, all converted from Martini-Henry arms — one from a carbine and three from rifles.

Martini-Metford Artillery Carbine Mark I

Approved on May 2, 1892, this carbine was converted from the Martini-Henry Mark I Artillery Carbine. Many of the Martini-Henry artillery carbine parts were used in the conversion without alteration; but the forend hook, nosecap, and forend required some alteration to suit the converted pattern.

In the conversion, many new components can be found, including the barrel, block, foresight and rearsight components, forend, bands, mainspring, rod nut, extractor, cleaning rod, and various screws.

Carbine length was 3 feet one inch, weight was 7 pounds one ounce, and barrel length was 21 inches.

Martini-Metford Artillery Carbine Mark II

The Martini-Metford Artillery Carbine Mark II, approved on October 11, 1893, was converted from a Martini-Henry Rifle Mark II.

The Mark II carbine differed from the Martini-Metford Artillery Carbine Mark I in that the butt swivel hole was plugged, the upper band was cut and drilled to receive the upper band screw and also had the lugs and sword bar removed, and the nosecap was shortened and drilled to receive the upper band screw.

Further, a number of additions were made to the Mark II Artillery Carbine — a rearsight cover and cover screws were installed, and a screw was added to the supper band.

Length of the carbine was 3 feet one inch, weight was 7 pounds one ounce, and barrel length was 21 inches.

Martini-Metford Artillery Carbine Mark II*

The Martini-Metford Artillery Carbine Mark II was approved on August 2, 1893, actually before the Mark II Artillery Carbine. The Mark II* also was converted from a Martini-Henry Rifle Mark II. This carbine never went into production since its designation was necessitated by the use of the Martini-Henry block, which was discontinued before actual production of this model.

Martini-Metford Artillery Carbine Mark III

The Martini-Metford Artillery Carbine Mark III, the last in this series, was approved on March 8, 1894. Converted from the Martini-Henry Rifle Mark III, this carbine had a different pattern knoxform, and attached the forend differently. Carbine length was 3 feet, one inch, with an total weight of 7 pounds 3 ounces. Barrel length was 21 inches.

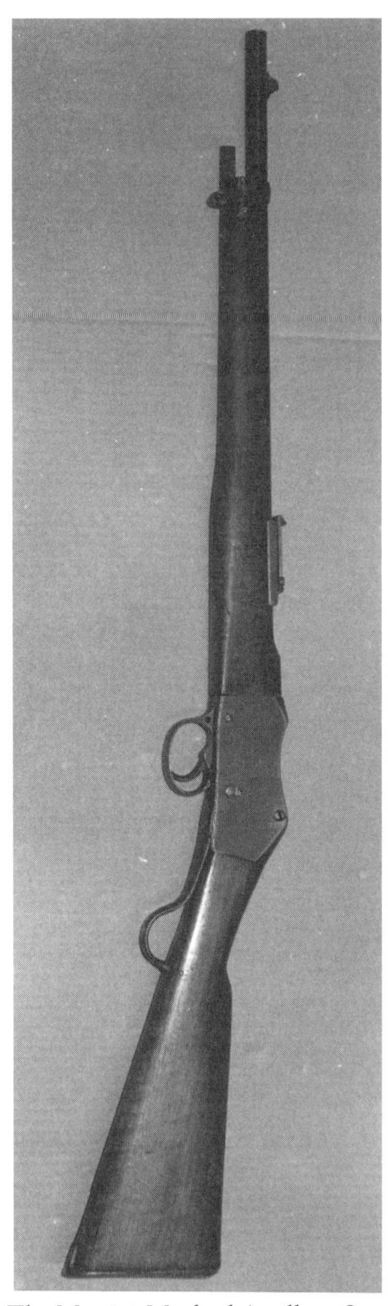

The Martini-Metford Artillery Carbine Mark III was approved on March 8, 1894.

Martini-Enfield Carbines

Like the earlier .303 Martini-Metford carbines, the .303 Martini-Enfield carbines were converted from various Martini-Henry .450 rifles and carbines.

In the Cavalry Carbine versions, the Mark I carbine traced its ancestry to a Martini-Henry .450 Mark II Rifle, while the Mark II carbine was converted from a Martini-Henry .450 Mark I Artillery Carbine.

On the Artillery Carbine side, the Mark I carbine was converted from a Martini-Henry .450 Mark III Rifle, the Mark II carbine from either a Martini-Henry .450 Mark III Rifle or a Martini-Henry .450 Mark I Artillery Carbine, and the Mark III carbine from a Martini-Henry .450 Mark II Rifle.

While confusing for the military historian now, the conversion program made use of those arms readily available and convertible at the time.

Martini-Enfield Cavalry Carbines

Three versions of the Martini-Enfield Cavalry Carbine were produced, all converted from Martini-Henrys — two from rifles and one from a carbine. The total production of the three marks, all converted at Royal Small Arms Factory at Enfield, was 6,955.

Martini-Enfield Cavalry Carbine Mark I

Approved on August 20, 1896, this carbine was converted from the Martini-Henry Mark II Rifle. Essentially the conversion consisted of fitting a .303-calibre Enfield rifled barrel to the arm. In addition, the carbine was fitted with a leather cover for the rearsight.

The rearsight leaf and cap were the same as those on the Lee-Enfield Cavalry Carbine, while the other parts in the weapon were common to the Martini-Metford Cavalry Carbine Mark III.

The Royal Small Arms Factory at Enfield made 5,990 Mark I conversions between 1898 and 1900.

Length of the carbine was 3 feet one inch, weight was 6 pounds 11 ounces, and barrel length was 21 inches.

Martini-Enfield Cavalry Carbine Mark II

The Martini-Enfield Cavalry Carbine Mark II was approved on November 7, 1901 and was converted from the Martini-Henry Artillery Carbine Mark I.

Fitting a .303-calibre Enfield rifled barrel to the arm was the most notable modification to the Martini-Henry from which it was converted.

Some 965 Mark II cavalry carbines were made at the Royal Small Arms Factory at Enfield during 1903 and 1904 for the government of New South Wales, Australia.

Length of the carbine was 3 feet one inch, weight was 6 pounds 11 ounces, and barrel length was 21 inches.

Martini-Enfield Cavalry Carbine Mark I*

This pattern was approved 7 August 1899, and was to be converted from a Martini-Henry Mark II Rifle. Apparently, no conversions to the Mark I* were ever produced.

Length of the carbine, as approved, was 3 feet one inch, weight was 6 pounds 11 ounces, and barrel length was 21 inches.

Martini-Enfield Artillery Carbines

Five versions of the Martini-Enfield Artillery Carbine were produced, all converted from Martini-Henry arms — three from rifles and two from carbines. The total production of the five marks, all converted at Royal Small Arms Factory at Enfield, was 90,118.

Martini-Enfield Artillery Carbine Mark I

Approved on January 4, 1896, this carbine was converted from the Martini-Henry Mark III Rifle.

The converted arm retained a number of parts from the Martini-Henry Mark III Rifle including various pins and screws, the body, butt, buttplate, guard, indicator, lever and its associated parts, upper band swivel, trigger parts, tumber, and stock bolt.

New components included the barrel, fore and rearsight parts, extractor, clearing rod, forend, nosecap, marking disk, striker, butt swivel, and mainspring.

The Royal Small Arms Factory at Enfield made 26,917 Mark I conversions in 1898 and 1899.

Length of the carbine was 3 feet one inch, weight was 7 pounds 4 ounces, and barrel length was 21 inches.

This Martini-Enfield Mark I Artillery Carbine went to New Zealand, according to the marking on the action.

Enfield converted this Martini-Enfield Artillery Carbine Mark I in 1895.

The markings designating the conversion information are on the left side of this Mark II Artillery Carbine, converted in 1898 at Enfield.

Martini-Enfield Artillery Carbine Mark II

The Martini-Enfield Cavalry Carbine Mark II was approved on December 6, 1897 and was converted from the Martini-Henry Artillery Carbine Mark I.

The parts to this carbine were common to the Martini-Enfield Artillery Carbine Mark I and the Martini-Metford Artillery Carbine Mark III with the exception of the body and forend.

The Royal Small Arms Factory at Enfield made 20,185 Mark II conversions in 1899 and 1900, while the Henry Rifle Barrel Co. (HRB) made 6,000 Mark II carbines in 1898.

Length of the carbine was 3 feet one inch, weight was 7 pounds 4 ounces, and barrel length was 21 inches.

The Martini-Enfield Mark II Artillery Carbine was approved on December 6, 1897.

Martini-Enfield Artillery Carbine Mark III

The Martini-Enfield Cavalry Carbine Mark II was approved on July 12, 1899 and was converted from the Martini-Henry Mark II Rifle.

The Mark III differed from the Martini-Metford Artillery Carbine Mark II in the rifling method (Enfield instead of Metford), the height and position of the foresight, and the height and gradations of the rearsight. This mark did not have any provision for a clearing rod.

The Royal Small Arms Factory at Enfield made 25,035 Mark III conversions between 1900 and 1904, while the BE Co. made 7,500 Mark III carbines between 1900 and 1902.

Length of the carbine was 3 feet one inch, weight was 7 pounds 4 ounces, and barrel length was 21 inches.

The Mark III version of the Martini-Enfield Artillery Carbine was approved on July 12, 1899.

Martini-Enfield Artillery Carbine Mark I*

This pattern was approved August 7, 1899, and was to be converted from a Martini-Henry Mark II Rifle. Apparently, no conversions to the Mark I* were ever produced.

Length of the carbine, as approved, was 3 feet one inch, weight was 6 pounds 11 ounces, and barrel length was 21 inches.

Martini-Enfield Artillery Carbine Mark II*

This pattern was approved August 7, 1899, and was converted from a Martini-Henry Artillery Carbine, Mark I or III.

While many of these converted carbines owed their parentage to a Martini-Henry Artillery Carbine, at least a small number of the conversions were upgrades of the Martini-Enfield Artillery Carbine Mark II. These latter arms show a nosecap replacement with no hole bored for a clearing rod, although the forend still had the rod hole in it.

The Royal Small Arms Factory at Enfield made 4,481 Mark II* conversions between 1900 and 1904.

Length of the carbine was 3 feet one inch, weight was 6 pounds 11 ounces, and barrel length was 21 inches.

The nosecap, bayonet stud and sling swivel are in evidence on this Mark III Artillery Carbine.

Lee-Metford Carbines

The development of the Lee-Metford and Lee-Enfield series of rifles was one strewn with obstacles for the British government. While the trend at the end of the nineteenth century was toward magazine rifles and higher powered and longer ranged cartridges, the British were still issuing their Martini-Henry rifle in .577/.450 calibre.

In 1883, the British organized a Small Arms Committee to deal with the improvement of the Martini-Henry rifle, but the committee also was charged with looking into the desirability of a magazine rifle for the British services.

Early in its deliberations, the committee determined that any magazine rifle should carry at least five rounds in the magazine, be of relatively simple design, not be inferior to the Martini-Henry rifle when used as a single loader, and be of comparable weight.

The committee examined many different designs of rifle, all of which were given exhaustive trials. There were three rifles which did not break down in any of the tests — the Owen Jones Magazine rifle; the Lee Magazine rifle, which had been improved at the Royal Small Arms Factory at Enfield; and the Improved Lee Rifle with the Bethel Burton magazine.

After more trials, the Owen Jones rifle was disqualified since it was expensive to manufacture and repair. That left the Lee Rifle with the Bethel Burton magazine and the Lee Magazine Rifle. These two firearms were placed into the final trials.

The Lee Magazine rifle used a magazine which was developed by James Paris Lee of Ilion, New York. The magazine was a metal case that was inserted into the action of the rifle from the bottom, feeding cartridges to the bolt to be stripped into the chamber. It had small ears at the top to retain the topmost of the five cartridges in the magazine.

The Bethel Burton magazine was a hopper which lay along the right side of the action when not in use. To operate the magazine, it was pushed inward so that the top projected over the body of the rifle. Only then could cartridges be loaded. It also held five rounds.

Ultimately, the Lee Magazine Rifle won the trials, but was not finally recommended since the British were still wrestling with the questions of what calibre the new rifle would take.

Finally, the British Small Arms Committee recommended a .303 calibre rifle for the service. Thus, in 1888, the Lee-Metford Magazine Rifle was born, mating a modified Lee action and magazine to rifling developed by William E. Metford. This was the beginning of a long line of successful rifles and carbines for the British that continued in service into the 1990s.

Lee-Metford Magazine Carbine, Mark I

The Lee-Metford Carbine Mark I.

Since mounted troops had difficulties carrying the long Lee-Metford rifle, it was decided to develop a shortened version for the cavalry. Approved September 29, 1894, the Lee-Metford Magazine Carbine, Mark I made its appearance.

With an overall length of 3 feet 4 inches, and a weight, empty, of 7 pounds 7 ounces, the carbine had a distinctly different appearance from the Lee-Metford Magazine Rifle, Mark II.

The carbine's barrel was 20.75 inches in length, but had the same internal dimensions as the rifle.

The bolt had an extension at the rear end, about one inch long, with two grooves for the safety catch. The bolt handle was bent so that it lay to the body of the carbine, and the knob of the lever was flattened at its top, so that it was less likely to snag in a saddle scabbard.

The cocking piece on the carbine was lengthened and fitted with a safety catch, with pin and spring. This assem-

The buttstock on the Lee-Metford Carbine Mark I incorporated a sling bar in place of a butt swivel. To the right of the sling bar is the brass marking disc, which was stamped with the arm's regimental details. The Enfield rondel and large Roman numeral "I" are just visible in the center of the buttstock.

bly allowed the whole action to be locked either at full cock or when the mainspring was eased.

The nosecap, combined with the upper band, had two wings to protect the foresight. It also was recessed at the back to receive and secure the handguard at that end. There was no provision for a bayonet stud or swivel on the nosecap.

The carbine's band, of oval form inside, had no shoulders and passed over both the handguard and forend. It was held in position by a band retaining spring, in the underside of the forend.

The wood handguard extended from the nosecap to the rearsight, and was secured at the rearsight by the band. When it was required to remove the handguard, the band screw was unscrewed, the band forced up to the nosecap, and the leaf of the rearsight raised. The handguard could then be taken off.

The butt plate on the carbine was of the same size and

shape as that of the Lee-Metford Magazine Rifle, Mark I*, but was made of delta metal instead of iron.

The action area remained much the same as that on the rifle, but it was necessary to alter the forend dimensions to fit the carbine

The buttstock also was smaller all over, except at the socket and butt plate ends. It had a sling bar let into its right side, fixed by two screws inserted from the left.

In addition, a sling loop was swiveled in a lump on the left side of the body, and was held in position by a pin driven into a hole in the body.

There was a recess provided in the butt for carrying an oil bottle and a pullthrough.

The trigger guard on the carbine had a loop for a magazine link across the front instead of the side. It also was recessed at the front end to clear the link and link loop on the magazine when it was placed on the carbine. Also, the link loop, which was brazed on across the case, was smaller since it had to pass through the guard.

The magazine was modified from its 10 round form, and made shallower, to hold six cartridges. This also caused the magazine spring to be made shorter. The magazine remained of similar shape to

The action on the Lee-Metford Carbine included a flattened bolt handle and a safety mechanism attached at the rear of the bolt handle.

the 10 round version, and was fitted to the case and platform in a similar manner to that of the Lee-Metford Magazine Rifle, Mark II.

The carbine was not provided with the volley sights.

The rearsight on the carbine, graduated for cordite, was marked from 600 yards to 2,000 yards on the leaf. On alternate sides of the leaf there were short lines, denoting intermediate 50 yard marks. The sight bed was graduated from 200 to 500 yards.

The rearsight slide was reversible, with the depth of the bar being the same as that of the "V" It was marked with a center line and two wind gauge lines.

Markings on the carbine were to be found on the left side of the butt socket and included the crown, VR, place of manufacture, year, and mark. Only RSAF Enfield manufactured the Lee-Metford carbine.

Lee-Enfield Carbines

With the introduction of the cordite cartridge and Enfield rifling came many conversions of arms which were likely to be useful to the British services in a new form. This included both rifles and carbines of the Lee-Metford series, as well as Martini-Henry rifles and carbines in .577/.450 calibre.

Martini-Henry Mark III rifles were first to be converted to use the new rifling and cartridge. Such rifles, in addition to being altered as rifles, also were converted into artillery carbines.

While such operations were taking place, the Volunteer and Militia units, as well as the Royal Engineers, Artillery and Ordnance Corps were suitably armed. The next step was the development of a new carbine using Enfield rifling for the Cavalry.

Lee-Enfield Magazine Carbine Mark I

Officially introduced on August 17, 1896, the Lee-Enfield Magazine Carbine, Mark I became part of the

The Lee-Enfield Carbine Mark I was introduced on August 17, 1896 and shared many of the attributes of its predecessor, the Lee-Metford Carbine.

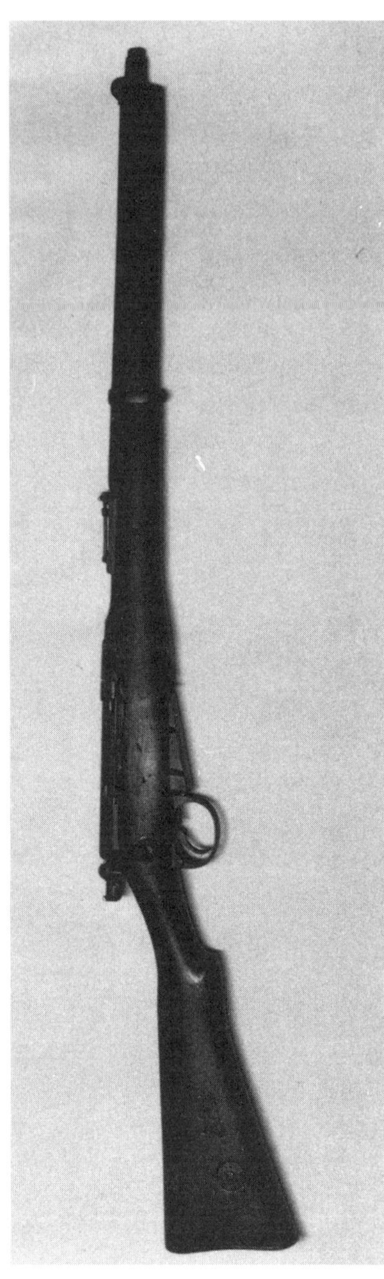

A change in rifling and the official cartridge served as the impetus for the development of the Lee-Enfield Carbine Mark I.

British arsenal of small arms. The chief differences from that of its predecessor, the Lee-Metford Magazine Carbine, Mark I were in the sighting, rifling, sling fittings, and the addition of a sight cover.

The major difference was one which could only be viewed by looking down the barrel. While the barrel length remained the same on the Lee-Enfield carbine, the rifling was the new Enfield 5-groove left hand twist necessary for the cordite cartridge.

Changing the rifling for the new cartridge also necessitated a change in the sights of the carbine, since the bullet trajectory would be different. The bed of the rearsight had gradations marked in hundred yard intervals from 200 to 500 yards, while the rearsight leaf was still graduated from 600 to 2,000 yards as was the earlier Lee-Metford carbine.

In addition the height and position of the barleycorn foresight was modified, as well as the height of the rearsight cap. The foresight again was placed .05 inches to the left of the center line of the axis of the bore, as was done on the

Lee-Enfield Magazine Rifle, Mark I.

The sling bar on the butt of the Lee-Metford carbine was omitted on this version, as was the D ring on the left of the receiver. The carbine was to be carried in a scabbard.

Markings on the carbine were placed on the left side of the butt socket and feature the crown, VR, year, L. E. C. I.

A leather rearsight cover was added to this carbine, which was held in pace by screws in either side of the forend. The fitting of the rearsight cover was applied to all other carbines then in service.

The magazine was retained in the six round version, as in the previous Lee-Metford carbine.

Lee-Enfield Magazine Carbine Mark I*

When the use of clearing rods were abolished on May 19, 1899, a change in the Lee-Enfield carbine became necessary in order to make it conform to pattern. Accordingly,

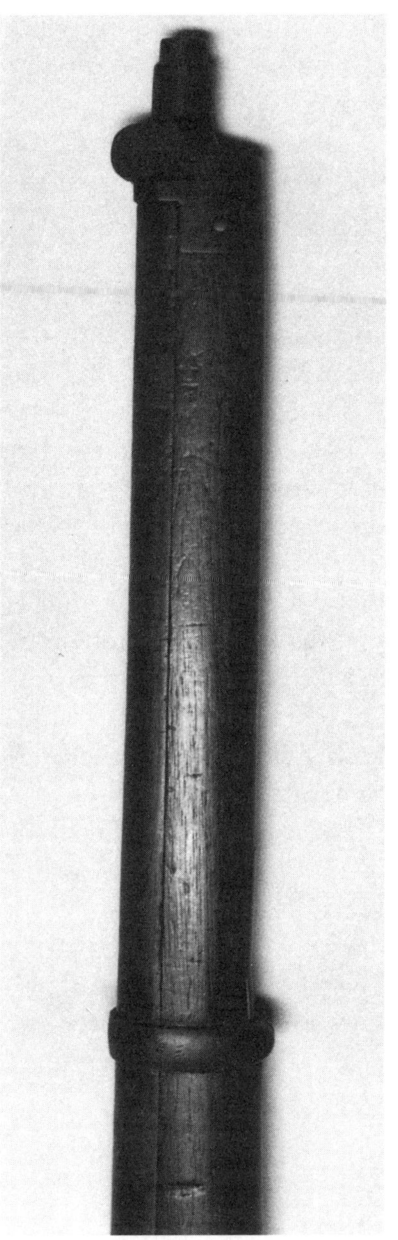

Abolition of the clearing rod brought about the Mark I* version of the Lee-Enfield Carbine.

on August 7, 1899, the Mark I* version was officially approved.

Abolition of the clearing rod meant a small change in the nosecap and forend of the carbine, which was accomplished in this mark. The most noticeable change in this mark was the deletion of the clearing rod hole.

The Mark I* carbine's other characteristics are the same as those on its predecessor — the flattened bolt handle remained the same, the furniture (with the exception of the modified forend) was unchanged, and the foresight and rearsight remained the same.

The carbine continued to be issued with the leather rearsight protector.

Markings continued to be placed on the left side of the butt socket, and featured the crown, VR, place of manufacture, year, and mark.

Lee Enfield Carbine (New Zealand)

This carbine, while officially announced in the British List of Changes, was never made

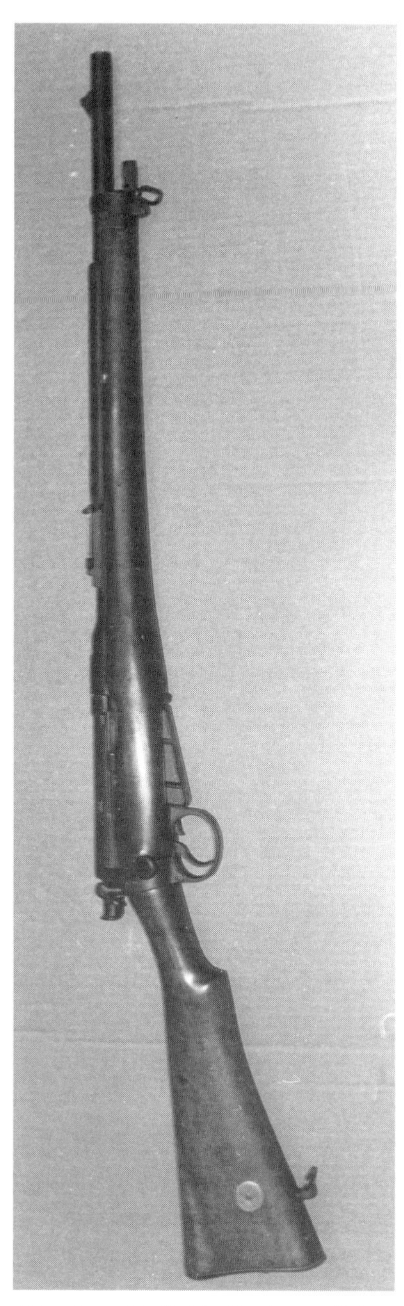

The Lee Enfield Carbine (New Zealand), a special contract arm, was not used by the British Army.

for British service. It only was made under special contract for the government of New Zealand.

As such, these New Zealand carbines will be found with a "NZ" surrounding a vertical broad arrow on the right butt socket. A New Zealand number and the date also will be stamped on the carbine.

The usual carbine markings of crown, VR, manufacturer, year and mark can be found on the left side of the butt socket.

Slightly heavier than the other Lee Enfield carbines at 7 pounds 8 ounces, this carbine had a heavier and slightly longer barrel. It was manufactured for use with the Pattern 1888 sword bayonet, and when the bayonet was affixed, the overall weight of the arm increased to 8 pounds 7.5 ounces.

Only 1,500 of these carbines were made at Royal Small Arms Factory at Enfield between 1901 and 1903.

The foresight of the carbine had protective wings and the rearsight was made and

The NZ stamping of the New Zealand government is just visible at the top of the socket on this carbine. The marking also included a broad arrow as part of its design.

marked like those of earlier carbines — the bed in hundred yard increments from 200 to 500 yards, and the leaf from 600 to 2,000 yards.

No leather sight protector was issued with this carbine.

Halfway through the production run, in 1902, the British changed the pattern on the rearsights of carbines, and this was also approved for the New Zealand pattern.

Sling swivels can be found on butt and the upper band of the carbine. The New Zealand carbine did not have a lower band, as did the Mark I and Mark I* carbines.

The furniture on the carbine is the same as on previous versions, with the exception of an altered handguard to accommodate the lack of a lower band.

Lee-Enfield Carbine (RIC)

One last conversion was in store for the Lee Enfield Carbine, this one done for the Royal Irish Constabulary (RIC) in 1905. The RIC order was placed for 10,000 carbines, and these were con-

The Lee-Enfield Carbine (RIC) was the last conversion done for this series of weapons.

This RIC was converted from a Lee-Enfield Carbine Mark I and shares many characteristics of the previous arm.

verted from the Lee-Metford and Lee-Enfield carbines then available.

The RIC carbine was to fix the Pattern 1888 bayonet, so the nosecap of the Cavalry Carbine was discarded and the RIC carbine fitted with one of the Lee-Enfield rifle variety. This necessitated some woodwork on the front of the forend. The grafting of a new piece of wood was readily apparent on RIC carbines.

In addition, the lower bands on the Lee-Metford and Lee-Enfield carbines were removed, and a wood patch was fitted in the recess for the band

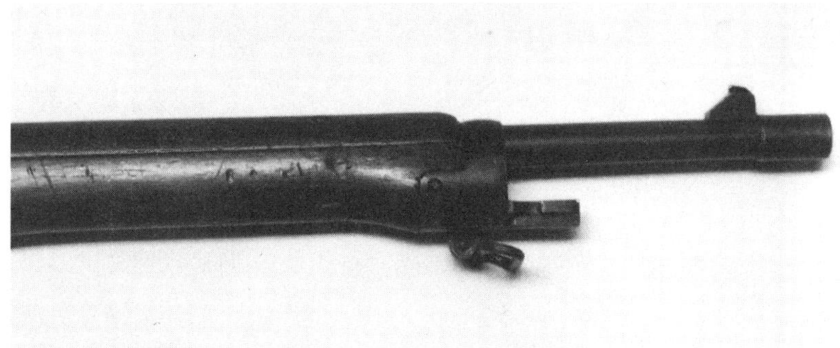

The forend of the RIC carbine required a modest amount of woodworking in order to be fitted with a nosecap to take the Pattern 1888 bayonet.

retaining catch.

The RIC carbine also is distinguishable by the inch-long collar fitted to the end of the carbine's barrel. This was done to allow the muzzle ring of the Pattern 1888 bayonet to engage the barrel properly.

The foresight on the RIC carbine is different from those it was converted from in that it uses a short ramp and barleycorn. The rearsight, however, did mirror the earlier carbine versions with a bed graduated from 200 to 500 yards in hundred yard increments, and a rearsight leaf from 600 to 2,000 yards.

Markings are on the left side of the butt socket and include the crown, VR, place of manufacture, yer, and carbine mark.

Number 5 Mark 1

The Number 5 Mark 1 was adopted on September 12, 1944.

The search for a shorter, lighter, handier rifle in World War II began soon after British forces found themselves crashing through thick jungles in the various outposts in southeast Asia.

At the time, British troopers were issued the old World War I standby, the Number 1 Mark III or Mark III* rifle. Production of the Number 4 Mark 1 rifles began in late 1941 and by early 1942 three different British factories, as well as two factories in North America would be making the arm. But it would be many months before such rifles flowed through the extensive (and very lengthy) logistical pipeline that led from the British Isles to the jungles below the equator.

The requests from troops for a shortened and lightened rifle continued. Ultimately, the result of the various tests, experiments and trials was the Number 5 Mark 1 rifle, an arm based on the Number 4 rifle.

While it had a brief life span in British service, the Number 5 rifle's development and use was interesting. It is included in this book since it is commonly known as the "Jungle Carbine," but never was officially designated as such. The Number 5 was issued to such diverse units as the British-equipped Polish Parachute Regiment and to units fighting communist insurgents in Malaya. Until recently, the Number 5 was in service with Indian and Pakastani Forces. Even the security forces at the Karachi airport were equipped with the Number 5 Mark 1 rifle.

The Indian, Australian and Canadian forces also wanted a short rifle during World War II. Of these, only Australia produced any appreciable quantity of rifles for testing. However, these were based on the Number 1 Mark III* rather than on the Number 4 Mark 1.

India also developed prototype Number 5 type rifles that were based on the Number 1 series. The Canadians took the same tack as the British and developed their lightened rifle around the Number 4. They also made initial steps toward producing the Number 5 rifle, but ultimately never did so.

The Number 5 Mark 1 rifle, commonly known as the Jungle Carbine due to its handy length and sporting appearance, first appeared in 1944 with the intent of ultimately supplanting the Number 4 rifle as the service arm for British forces. Alas, the next few years of production in Great Britain and actual use around the world, as well as improvements in the field of arms and ammunition, were to push that objective beyond the reach of the Number 5 rifle.

Number 5 rifles were produced at Britain's Royal Ordnance Factory at Fazakerley near Liverpool, and at the BSA factory at Shirley, outside Birmingham.

Adopted officially by the British on September 12, 1944, the Number 5 Mark 1 was five inches shorter overall, at 39.5 inches, than the Number 4 rifle. In addition, the barrel of the Number 5 Mark 1 — including its distinctive flash eliminator — was only 20.5 inches, com-

Markings designating the model, date and place of manufacture were engraved on the left side of the Number 5 Mark 1 receiver. These marks can sometimes be found on the left butt socket on early models of the weapon.

pared to the Number 4's barrel of 25 inches.

The official weight of the rifle was 7 lb. 2.5 oz., which was a savings of almost two pounds over the Number 4 rifle's weight.

The action on the Number 5 Mark 1 rifle was very similar to that on the Number 4 Mark 1, with the exception that lightening cuts were made in the Number 5 receiver to reduce weight. These are most noticeable at the left rear of the receiver above the safety catch, and on the right rear where the bolt handle turns down. Essentially, this means that the Number 5 receiver is slightly less robust than that of the Number 4 rifle, yet it still was of sufficient strength to handle the .303 British round.

The charger bridge on the Number 5 rifle was the same as that on the Number 4, being made of two pieces instead of a single large bridge. The trim contour of the Number 4 rifle's charger bridge can be seen mirrored in the Number 5 rifle. The same ejector screw used on the Number 4 rifle, in the left center of the receiver, was used on the Number 5 Mark 1.

The bolt and bolthead of the Number 5 again provide a mirror image to that of the Number 4, with the exception that Number 5 bolt bodies had hollowed out bolt handles to make them slightly lighter. This hollow bolt knob did not adversely affect the functioning of the action. Rebuilt rifles may be found with sold bolt handles on bolts originally intended for use with the Number 4 rifle.

And as with the Number 4 series, the Number 5 Mark 1 rifle's bolt had the advantage of having one of four different bolt head sizes affixed to it. The bolt head was issued in sizes 0, 1, 2 and 3, with the size being stamped on the top of the bolt head. A zero-designated bolt head was the shortest in length, while the 3 bolt head was the longest. When a rifle's headspace was too large, an armourer only had to increase the size of the bolt head to cure the problem.

While the Number 5 rifle's barrel was only 20.5 inches long, including the flash eliminator, it still was of the same stiff contour as that on the Number 4 rifle. However, it did have a number of lightening cuts made in the metal around the knox form to reduce its overall weight. The Number 5 rifles were fitted with five groove barrels of concentric form, making one turn in 10 inches, left hand twist. The width of the rifling grooves was .0936 inches, while the depth was .005 inch.

The length of the Number 5 barrel gave the rifle a sighting radius of 23-1/4 inches.

The rearsight of the Number 5 rifle was virtually identical to the Mark 1 milled micrometer rearsight first used on the Number 4 Mark 1 rifle. However, the graduations on the Number 5 rearsight were engraved to 800 yards, while the Number 4 rearsight was graduated to 1,300 yards.

The Number 5 rearsight was hinged at the rear of the receiver on a crosspin which engaged two small projection ears. When folded forward, the rearsight fit into a recess in the top of the receiver. The chief means of sighting when the rearsight was folded forward was the battle aperture, which was sighted for 300 yards with the bayonet fixed. When it was necessary to engage targets beyond 300 yards, the sight was raised and was locked in place by a spring and plunger.

Elevation was adjusted on the rearsight through a screw wheel at the top of the sight, but there was no adjustment for windage.

A Mark 2 rearsight for the Number 5 rifle came into use late in World War II, part of the move toward cutting costs and speeding manufacturing processes. The Mark 2 rearsight was a stamped steel affair, strangely reminiscent of the Mark 3 rearsight manufactured for some Number 4 series rifles earlier in the war.

This rearsight was a sheet metal pressing which attached to the same crosspin as the Mark 1 rearsight. Activation of the Mark 2's aperture slide, which also was a pressing, was by a spring and lever protruding from the right side of the sight.

The foresight on the Number 5 was a dovetailed blade, much like that on the Number 1 and Number 4 series rifles. A second mark of foresight also was issued, which featured a lengthened platform at the back of the blade.

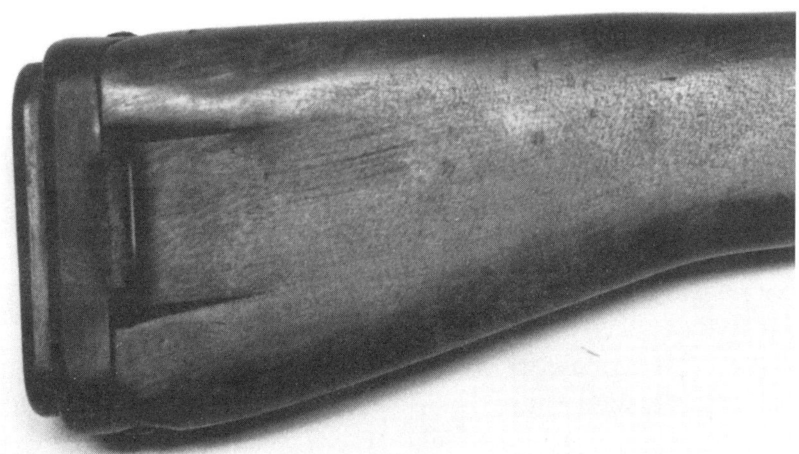

The buttstock on the Number 5 Mark 1 was designed to be fitted with a rubber butt pad that incorporated a sling bar.

Unlike the earlier Lee Enfield models, which used a foresight base block pinned to the barrel, the Number 5 rifle secured its foresight blade into a base block built as an integral part of the flash eliminator. The block had two foresight protection ears in the form of open half circles on either side to protect the blade.

The flash eliminator itself was 3-1/2 inches long and was attached to the barrel by two cross pins set into horizontal cuts. It was necessitated on the rifle since various firing tests showed the muzzle flash to be excessive.

The flash eliminator also carried a bayonet stud, to which the new Number 5 knife bayonet could be affixed.

The finish of the Number 5 Mark 1 rifle was similar to that of the Number 4 rifle. Metal parts were finished with an oil blacking process, similar to parkerizing, but imparting to the metal a deep black, glossy finish. The woodwork of the rifle was finished in the traditional method with linseed oil.

The forend on the Number 5 was perhaps one its most distinctive features, giving the rifle the look and feel of a sporting rifle. Instead of a full-length forend like that on the Number 1 Mark III rifle, or the forend of the Number 4 Mark 1 which extended to within 2.5 inches of the muzzle, the Number 5 Mark 1 forend extended just under three inches past the middle band. It thus gave the impression of a half-stocked rifle in the sporting tradition. Numbering the forend with the rifle's serial number was approved on November 14, 1945.

Early versions of the Number 5 rifle had the front of the forend finished by being tapered and rounded off. But by mid-1944, a concern developed that moisture might get into the forend woodwork through the unprotected end. Thus, a request for the development of an end cap for the forend was made.

The first end cap for the Number 5 was a curved model of thin metal that enclosed the rounded tip of the forend, and was secured in place by a cross pin set through the forend. After several months of fabrication, it was decided that this form of end cap presented too many manufacturing difficulties for so small a part, and a new design was developed.

The second metal end cap for the rifle was more angular than the first model, with an nearly squared off end profile. However, after about a year this model end cap also was discontinued and rifles reverted to a tapered and rounded end.

The handguard for the Number 5 rifle was longer than its Number 4 counterpart, having a horizontal slot cut into it to accept the barrel band slightly over an inch from its muzzle end. There was only a single handguard on the Number 5.

A barrel band encircled the handguard and forend, affixed by a standard cross screw. A standard pattern sling swivel was fitted to the screw.

The butt stock was furnished in three lengths for this rifle — long, normal and short. Each version was stamped to indicate its length, although in many instances, the normal lengths were left unmarked.

The flash eliminator on the Number 5 Mark 1 was very distinctive at the time, and a departure from previous British long arms.

The butt stock, while similar to that of the Number 4 and Number 1 series of rifles, was of a thicker cross section at the cheek, and with a less-pronounced grip area. But the most noticeable feature of the butt stock was its rubber butt pad and sling swivel attachment.

Instead of the standard brass or pot metal butt plate of the Number 4 rifle, which was affixed with two large screws, the Number 5 rifle used and entirely different form of butt plate. This was a solid rubber butt pad held in place by a metal frame. The frame covered the entire end of the butt stock, and was held in place by a double headed screw which ran vertically through the butt stock.

The purpose of the heavy rubber butt pad was to dampen some of the excess recoil which developed from shortening the barrel and lightening the rifle.

Since the Number 5 rifle did not shoot as well as the Number 4 when using sling tension, due to the lesser weight of the rifle, it was decided that the lower swivel of the Number 5 be designed only for carrying purposes. Accordingly, a provision was incorporated into the design of the butt pad frame for a sling swivel bar. This necessitated removing a small amount of wood from the butt stock so that the sling would be able to be fitted properly.

The trigger, sear, sear spring, and magazine catch were of the same type as that found on the Number 4 rifle series, as was the bolt release catch assembly.

The trigger guard was of a slightly different type, with some of its metal removed for lightness, although it was the same length as that on the Number 4 rifle. The Number 5 trigger guard also had the trigger pinned to it as on the Number 4 Mark 1 and Mark 1* rifles.

The magazine on the Number 5 was basically the same as that used on Number 4 rifles, and would interchange freely. Numbering the magazine to the rifle's serial number was approved on June 3, 1946.

Specifications

Snider Artillery Carbine Mark II*
Barrel length 24 inches
Caliber .577
Rifling 5 grooves of progressive depth, 1 turn in 48 inches
Date Adopted May 2, 1867
Manufacturer Royal Small Arms Factory, Enfield

Snider Artillery Carbine Mark III
Barrel length 24 inches
Caliber .577
Rifling 5 grooves of progressive depth, 1 turn in 48 inches
Date Adopted 1869
Manufacturer Royal Small Arms Factory, Enfield

Snider Artillery Carbine Mark IV
Barrel length 22.5 inches
Caliber .577
Rifling 3 grooves of progressive depth, 1 turn in 48 inches
Date Adopted 1891
Manufacturer Royal Small Arms Factory, Enfield

Snider Cavalry Carbine Mark II*
Barrel length 19 inches
Caliber .577
Rifling 5 grooves of progressive depth, 1 turn in 48 inches
Date Adopted May 2, 1867
Manufacturer Royal Small Arms Factory, Enfield

Snider Cavalry Carbine Mark III
Barrel length 19 inches
Caliber .577
Rifling 5 grooves of progressive depth, 1 turn in 48 inches
Date Adopted 1869
Manufacturer Royal Small Arms Factory, Enfield

Snider Yeomanry Carbine Mark I
Barrel length 19 inches
Caliber .577
Rifling 5 grooves of progressive depth, 1 turn in 48 inches
Date Adopted July 19, 1880
Manufacturer Royal Small Arms Factory, Enfield

Martini-Henry Carbine Mark I (Cavalry Carbine)
Barrel length 21.375 inches
Caliber .450
Rifling 7 grooves right hand twist, 1 turn in 22 inches
Date Adopted December 1, 1877
Manufacturer Royal Small Arms Factory, Enfield

Martini-Henry Garrison Artillery Carbine Mark I
Barrel length 21.375 inches
Caliber .450
Rifling 7 grooves right hand twist, 1 turn in 22 inches
Date Adopted April 9, 1878
Manufacturer Royal Small Arms Factory Enfield

Martini-Henry Artillery Carbine Mark I
Barrel length 21.375 inches
Caliber .450
Rifling 7 grooves right hand twist, 1 turn in 22 inches
Date Adopted July 21, 1879
Manufacturers Royal Small Arms Factory, Enfield; Birmingham Small Arms and Metal Co. Ltd.

Martini-Henry Artillery Carbine Mark II
Barrel length 21.437 inches
Caliber .450
Rifling 7 grooves right hand twist, 1 turn in 22 inches
Date Adopted August 18, 1891
Manufacturer Royal Small Arms Factory, Enfield

Martini-Henry Artillery Carbine Mark III
Barrel length 21.375 inches
Caliber .450
Rifling 7 grooves right hand twist, 1 turn in 22 inches
Date Adopted September 2, 1891
Manufacturer Royal Small Arms Factory, Enfield

Martini-Metford Cavalry Carbine Mark I

Barrel length 21 inches
Caliber .303
Rifling Metford, 7 grooves left hand twist, 1 turn in 10 inches
Date Adopted May 2, 1892
Manufacturer Henry Rifle Barrel Company

Martini-Metford Cavalry Carbine Mark II

Barrel length 21 inches
Caliber .303
Rifling Metford, 7 grooves left hand twist, 1 turn in 10 inches
Date Adopted May 2, 1892
Manufacturer Henry Rifle Barrel Company

Martini-Metford Cavalry Carbine Mark I* and II*

Barrel length 21 inches
Caliber .303
Rifling Metford, 7 grooves left hand twist, 1 turn in 10 inches
Date Adopted December 5, 1892
Manufacturer Henry Rifle Barrel Company; Royal Small Arms Factory, Enfield

Martini-Metford Cavalry Carbine Mark III

Barrel length 21 inches
Caliber .303
Rifling Metford, 7 grooves left hand twist, 1 turn in 10 inches
Date Adopted July 29, 1892
Manufacturer Henry Rifle Barrel Company; Royal Small Arms Factory, Enfield

Martini-Metford Artillery Carbine Mark I

Barrel length 21 inches
Caliber .303
Rifling Metford, 7 grooves left hand twist, 1 turn in 10 inches
Date Adopted May 2, 1892
Manufacturer Henry Rifle Barrel Company; Royal Small Arms Factory, Enfield

Martini-Metford Artillery Carbine Mark II

Barrel length 21 inches
Caliber .303
Rifling Metford, 7 grooves left hand twist, 1 turn in 10 inches
Date Adopted October 11, 1893
Manufacturer Royal Small Arms Factory, Enfield

Martini Metford Artillery Carbine Mark II*

Barrel length 21 inches
Caliber .303
Rifling Metford, 7 grooves left hand twist, 1 turn in 10 inches
Date Adopted August 2, 1893
Manufacturer Royal Small Arms Factory, Enfield

Martini-Metford Artillery Carbine Mark III

Barrel length 21 inches
Caliber .303
Rifling Metford, 7 grooves left hand twist, 1 turn in 10 inches
Date Adopted March 8, 1894
Manufacturer Henry Rifle Barrel Company; Royal Small Arms Factory, Enfield

Martini-Enfield Cavalry Carbine Mark I

Barrel length 21 inches
Caliber .303
Rifling Enfield, 5 grooves, left hand twist, 1 turn in 10 inches
Date Adopted August 20, 1896
Manufacturer Royal Small Arms Factory, Enfield

Martini-Enfield Cavalry Carbine Mark II

Barrel length 21 inches
Caliber .303
Rifling Enfield, 5 grooves, left hand twist, 1 turn in 10 inches
Date Adopted November 7, 1901
Manufacturer Royal Small Arms Factory, Enfield

Martini-Enfield Cavalry Carbine Mark I*

Barrel length	21 inches
Caliber	.303
Rifling	Enfield, 5 grooves, left hand twist, 1 turn in 10 inches
Date Adopted	August 7, 1899
Manufacturer	Royal Small Arms Factory, Enfield

Martini-Enfield Artillery Carbine Mark I

Barrel length	21 inches
Caliber	.303
Rifling	Enfield, 5 grooves, left hand twist, 1 turn in 10 inches
Date Adopted	January 4, 1896
Manufacturer	Royal Small Arms Factory, Enfield; Henry Rifle Barrel Company

Martini-Enfield Artillery Carbine Mark II

Barrel length	21 inches
Caliber	.303
Rifling	Enfield, 5 grooves, left hand twist, 1 turn in 10 inches
Date Adopted	December 6, 1897
Manufacturer	Royal Small Arms Factory, Enfield; Henry Rifle Barrel Company

Martini-Enfield Artillery Carbine Mark III

Barrel length	21 inches
Caliber	.303
Rifling	Enfield, 5 grooves, left hand twist, 1 turn in 10 inches
Date Adopted	July 12, 1899
Manufacturer	Royal Small Arms Factory, Enfield; BE Company

Martini-Enfield Artillery Carbine Mark I*

Barrel length	21 inches
Caliber	.303
Rifling	Enfield, 5 grooves, left hand twist, 1 turn in 10 inches
Date Adopted	August 7, 1899
Manufacturer	Royal Small Arms Factory, Enfield

Martini-Enfield Artillery Carbine Mark II*

Barrel length 21 inches
Caliber .303
Rifling Enfield, 5 grooves, left hand twist, 1 turn in 10 inches
Date Adopted August 7, 1899
Manufacturer Royal Small Arms Factory, Enfield

Lee-Metford Magazine Carbine Mark I

Barrel length 20.75 in.
Caliber .303 in.
Rifling Metford, 7 grooves left hand twist, 1 turn in 10 inches
Date Adopted September 29, 1894
Manufacturer Royal Small Arms Factory, Enfield

Lee-Enfield Magazine Carbine, Mark I

Barrel length 20.75 in.
Caliber .303 in.
Rifling Enfield, 5 grooves, left hand twist, 1 turn in 10 inches
Date Adopted August 17, 1896
Manufacturer Royal Small Arms Factory, Enfield

Lee-Enfield Magazine Carbine, Mark I*

Barrel length 20.75 in.
Caliber .303 in.
Rifling Enfield, 5 grooves, left hand twist, 1 turn in 10 inches
Date Adopted August 7, 1899
Manufacturer Royal Small Arms Factory, Enfield

Lee-Enfield Magazine Carbine (New Zealand)

Barrel length 21 in.
Caliber .303 in.
Rifling Enfield, 5 grooves, left hand twist, 1 turn in 10 inches
Date Adopted May 30, 1900
Manufacturer Royal Small Arms Factory, Enfield

Lee-Enfield Carbine (RIC)

Barrel length	20.75 in.
Caliber	.303 in.
Rifling	Enfield, 5 grooves, left hand twist, 1 turn in 10 inches
Date Adopted	1903
Manufacturer	Royal Small Arms Factory, Enfield; Birmingham Small Arms Company

Number 5 Mark 1

Barrel length	20.5 in.
Caliber	.303 in.
Rifling	Enfield, 5 grooves, left hand twist, 1 turn in 10 inches
Date Adopted	September 12, 1944
Manufacturer	BSA Shirley; Fazakerley

Acknowledgments

There are many friendly, helpful individuals whom one meets when researching a book, and this one has been no different. I especially want to thank Bob Washburn, Bob Maze and Larry Grimm, all in the United States for their assistance and support, while in Great Britain, Chris Law was of special help. These individuals either supplied information or allowed their collections to be photographed, or both. To them all, my grateful thanks.

I also owe a debt to the late Dennis Lewis for his friendship and support on this project. Dennis was to be a co-author of this book, but an automobile accident in 1997 cut short his life before we had the chance to begin collaborating on the manuscript. I'm pleased to include the carbine material from Dennis' book, *Martini-Henry .450 Rifles & Carbines*, also published by Excalibur Publications, in this work. Dennis, we miss you.

About the Author

Alan M. Petrillo, a writer by profession, is an avid student of British history, especially relating to military subjects. He is well respected in the field of British firearms and their development.

Among his writing accomplishments are his editing of books on firearms and military history subjects, and publication of firearms-related articles in periodicals such as *Military History* magazine, *Rifle* magazine, and *World War II*.

Petrillo is the author of four other books on British firearms:

- *British Service Rifles and Carbines 1888-1900*
- *The Lee Enfield Number 1 Rifles*
- *The Lee Enfield Number 4 Rifles*
- *The Number 5 Jungle Carbine.*

All are published by Excalibur Publications.